Between Tampax
and
Depends

HAROLD J ANGER SR
14 ROBINSON ST
SILVER CREEK NY 14136-1517

Between Tampax and Depends

ISBN # 978-1-4414509-7-5

Copyright ©2012 by Bertamae Anger Ives

Cover Illustration by Charles Bruce

Additional copies are available from Amazon.com
or the author.

Visit me on the web at

www.bertamaeives.com

AuntBertieAnger@gmail.com

*In loving memory of my husband of
twenty-six years, Reverend Richard
Henry Ives, whose friendly persuasion,
teasing and loving changed my
perspective on many things.*

*Many thanks to my friend, Jeanne Treat, for her editing
advice and to the Northside Writers Group for their input.*

Bertamae Anger Ives

Bertamae is a teacher and organist who traveled extensively within the United States and to eighteen countries to work with relief organizations. She is an award winning author who enjoys writing and humor. She writes for the "My View" Column of the Buffalo News, is the author of "Ring in the Holidays" and a contributor to "Doing Good For Goodness Sake".

Between Tampax
and
Depends

Inspiration for the mature woman. A
smattering of personal experiences mixing
humor with poignant insights, designed to
bless and entertain.

Contents

When In Doubt, Don't

Section Five – Helping People

Wrapup

Introduction

A Mature Dilemma

I'm between Tampax and Depends; a mature older gal past fifty. I refuse to grow old graciously. I'm fighting it every inch of the way.

My first clue was at the beauty shop a few years back. The girl scrubbed my hairline along my left cheek. Vainly she tried to scrub that large dark brown spot away. "I guess that isn't dirt, Mrs. Ives. What is it? A birthmark, perhaps?"

Like an aging ship, every two or three years, I need to be dry-docked at the dermatologist office for three to five appointments. The doctor burns and cuts with acid or liquid nitrogen - moles, tags, and ghastly lumps that keep reappearing. My crop of warts shows up in the strangest places: in between my toes, in my armpits, and behind my ears.

I fear that I'll wake some morning with a large mole with a gray hair blossoming on the end of my nose. "Damn that magnifying mirror! It catches everything." It's bad enough to know that a stray hair is growing, but quite another to see it well enough to grasp it.

My "birthday suit" has so many brown liver spots that I look like a second grader's dot-to-dot workbook. Discolored, transparent textured skin reveals my varicose veins. This is God's way of keeping me humble.

I'm grateful for such minor problems, when friends and relatives are facing debilitating life threatening strokes and cancers. Truly, I can live with such trivial problems! "Go ahead God, and tattoo me with liver spots and moles. I await my new crop of barnacles with joy. I'm your unique antique!"

Transitions

Why Can't I Be Sexy?

Other people look attractive, but not me! I have been trying to look sexy or at least glamorous for years.

At sixteen my parents planned a Blow out Birthday Party! They invited neighbors, relatives and my friends from high school. They purchased a stunning dress, with shoes dyed to match, and the house was filled with flowers. My chance to impress everyone was here. I impressed them all right. One hour before the festive event I tripped over the dog, spraining my ankle. My elegant celebration was half over when I arrived in jeans with crutches.

Back in the 60s' I watched TV personalities and movie starlets step from their limousine holding a fur muff. That year my husband surprised me with one. Clutching a black seal muff when you're eight months pregnant just adds to your girth.

The following year I decided a fancy red velvet dress for special occasions would be great. But it's hard being distinctive when you can't leave your home without dragging a diaper bag. They don't come in red.

Perhaps a slinky black beaded dress would do it. One hundred and twenty dollars poorer, my results were the same. Our couples club attended a dinner at a ritzy hotel. Yes, Calamity Jane wore the slinky dress - with my arm in a sling because of a tennis elbow.

In 1985, my extra cash went for a special hat for my son's Boy Scout God and Country Award ceremony. This one-of-a-kind brimmed hat was just what I needed. Then my dermatologist called and said he had a cancellation that same day. He decided to remove moles from my face. I kept saying, "Yes." At the end of the session to my surprise several bandages were put on. At the impressive ceremony people asked if I had been in an auto accident because three Band-Aids adorned my face. Nobody noticed my new hat.

13

I'm doomed to going through life gaining attention for all the wrong reasons.

Life in the new millennium is different. I have to hurry to be glamorous. Soon it will be forever too late. Why? It's hard to appear sexy or fetching in orthopedic shoes when you're awaiting a hip replacement.

Naked in the Hall

I attended a Write to Publish Conference in the midwest at an Evangelical School in Illinois. The crowd was close to three hundred people. So as a late comer, I was assigned to a corner room on the third floor of the old women's dorm, which lacked air conditioning.

The conference proved to be a succession of blistering days with heat of 94-96 degrees. So I slept without the damp confines of a nightgown.

When I woke up in the morning, it was pretty quiet at 6:30 A.M. I was just two doors from the rest room so I streaked down the hall in response to nature's call. I left my door wide open because the night latch was still on. When I returned a breeze had blown my door shut!

I knocked on a friend's door and hid my birthday suit, putting my one shoulder and my chin in the opening. "Hi Burnice. Sorry to bother you so early..." My friend was packed, her bags were locked, and the room was stripped of all linen. A cab tooted impatiently for her outside her window. I pleaded, "Can I use your phone to call security?"

She let me in. "Sure go ahead but what are you going to do when they get here?" she said with a giggle.

"Please, please loan me a..."

"I'm already late for my train. Use the phone and then lock the door when you leave."

I phoned while she gathered her bags and left for the elevator. Running back to the restroom, I looked for anything. Even a dirty towel would do. No luck!

Maybe I could plaster my body with wet paper towels. Forget that! They would not stay in place. I had gained weight recently. It would take two dozen towels to cover me. Perhaps wrapping myself in toilet paper like a mummy would work. But I needed my arms free to wrap myself. The paper slipped off my hips. *I'm running out of time, they'll be here any minute!*

Thank God, I eyed the shower curtain. I sprinted back to Burnice's room for a chair, then raced back to unhook sixteen rings and wrap myself in white plastic. Nonchalantly sitting on the floor, the door at the end of our wing opened.

Security had thoughtfully sent a female guard, with a ring of keys as big as a watermelon. I gave out a sigh of relief. This proved to be a mixed blessing! She began to snicker and burst out laughing. "Are you Mrs. Ives? You know the rules here on campus. Have you been drinking?" She then bent low over me to smell my breath. "Did you borrow your designer dress from the shower stall?" She dropped the keys. They hit the floor like a bowling ball.

Immediately, three doors opened. People poured into the hall and commented. "What's so funny?" "What's going on?" "Oh, my!" "She's dressed appropriately for the weather."

"Hey Helen, don't you think this is a newsworthy event, for the conference daily paper? How about the 'Bare Facts Column? Right girls?"

I took fifteen minutes of teasing before the guard's fumbling fingers found the right match for my door.

The panic I felt and the ribbing I took taught me an important lesson - if I ever decide to become a streaker again, I should take my keys!

Transparent Woman

(my experience as a new widow)

The phone doesn't ring
The house is quiet

Friends tiptoe around me
Afraid to mention his name.

At a party, eyes pass over me like
I was an insect on the wall.

Harassing phone calls in the wee
Hours disturb my slumber.

People I danced with, ate with, golfed with,
Pretend I don't exist.

I am a silent reminder that
We are all vulnerable to that final call.

Diabetic Heaven

Hello!
Is that you Bertamae? an angel said to me.
Everyone's surprised you made it!
You've longed to be here for years
…and years.

Banana splits are straight ahead.
Pecan pie is on the left.
Sundaes are behind the blueberry pies.
On the left near the milkshake fountains, mountains of 6-
layer birthday cakes await you.
High calorie drinks are around the throne of God himself.
Strawberry tequilas are free.
Help yourself!

See what the Lord has provided for you!
You got here somehow…
Though He noticed you did a lot of cheating on your diet.
When it comes to overdoing it……
Snitching truffles regularly is a sin!

We have mountains of candy bars,
puddles of apple sauce,
lakes of maple syrup over potato pancakes.
Licorice trees are near the rainbow.
Gardens of nuts are growing in whipped cream clouds.
Hershey kisses hang from them.

Stones are made of hard candy.
Sink holes of hot fudge to dip Girl Scout cookies in.
Fences of candy canes guard bowls of English trifle that
wait for you!
Candied fruit petals adorn the flowers.

Go ahead!
Climb mountains of fudge fenced in with caramels.

Before you get started, thank the Lord.
It is time to enjoy your sweet rewards.

I Know I'm Fifty Because...

I know I'm fifty because... I no longer feel safe. Yesterday I saw a squad car waiting beside me at the signal light. With stunned surprise, I stared into the fuzzy bearded face of a young man who looked about sixteen. He might be the same age as my son. This green youth is my protection?

I know I'm fifty because... At the optician's, I listened to a sales pitch exalting the benefits of trifocals delivered to me by a fledgling salesmen. He had a condescending attitude, and never in his short life had he ever worn glasses. Steaming with resentment, I rammed on a pair of glasses, wrote the check, and fled the store. Out in the mall, my stomach was churning and my vision was blurring.

"Mrs. Ives," yelled the youngster in hot pursuit. "Your vision is blurred because you have my demonstration glasses on!"

Returning home I entered the house and discovered the extension phone off the hook and a cup of cold coffee waiting for me. Over the hill is bad enough, but my forgetfulness means I'm slipping into the sea of senility.

I know I'm fifty because... At the ticket booth for the movies, I keep hoping that someone behind the counter will argue with me because I look "too young" for the senior discount price. So far, that has not happened!

I know I'm fifty because... My get-up-and-go has deserted me! Touring a mall with fifty seven stores sounds like work to me. Sneaking in an afternoon siesta has suddenly become a wonderful idea.

I know I'm fifty because... When teenagers come to my door and offer to shovel my sidewalk, they must think I am to too frail to accomplish it myself.

I know I'm fifty because... When traveling alone nobody tries to pick me up. I'm too heavy and too old!

What use to be "Hi Babe" from a friendly truck driver is now, "Hey, lady, where is 390 south?"

I know I'm fifty because… After my splendid vacation, three inches of exposed white roots appeared on my head where Clairol ash blond should be. That nervy waitress suggested the Wednesday Senior Citizen Special.

I know I'm fifty because… The flashy fall previews are not designed for mature figures. I need clothes that will camouflage my aging anatomy. Finding a swimming suit is a bigger challenge than I imagined. One day shopping, I pushed through the hangers franticly looked for my size; only to spy two red Ping–Pong balls with four yellow straps dangling from them.

I know I'm fifty because… The "chick of the 50's" who used to wear four inch spiked heels all day now looks for a wedged heel shoe with a strap across the ankle. The young woman of the past that ran through a park or dashed through a department store now searches for an elevator. I watch with envy at O'Hare Airport, when oldsters ride in an escort cart from the parking lot to their departure gate.

I know I'm fifty because… At the high school open house night, I approached a mature man with a suit and tie who was my age. He looked intelligent and competent. Immediately, I introduced myself and launched into my son's problems with chemistry. He interrupted me to say, "That's interesting, but I'm Jim's dad. The teacher is the 'kid' with the Adam's apple and the red tie standing near the bulletin board."

I know I'm fifty!

Rolling Stone - a quote by Allen

My hairdresser summed it up. "You know you are over fifty when you're on your fourth dog, and you have gone from the 'ROLLING Stones to gall stones!"

Mr. Allen Mascia

The Five Thousand Dollar Makeup Mirror
(my friend Jeanne tells this story)

When I was in my mid-fifties, my eyes were starting to fail. I purchased a lighted magnifying mirror to help me put on my makeup. What a mistake! When I peered in the glass for the first time, I noticed out of control eyebrows, blotches, wrinkles, fat pouches around my eyes, and a hair in my chin that looked like a piece of fishing line.

"Why didn't you tell me I looked like this?" I asked my husband.

"I'm not answering that," he said.

I was shocked at my appearance. When I looked in the mirror, I felt like saying, "Mom, is that you?"

I went to a Merle Norman studio and had my eyebrows shaped. Then I visited a plastic surgery practice that promised to restore my youth. I turned over $2,000 for a series of 6 treatments – 3 chemical peels and 3 laser resurfacing sessions. The peels were uncomfortable but the

27

laser treatments were downright painful. I remember thinking that the only difference betwen this and torture was that I could get up off the table. They did work, however. Twelve weeks later, my skin was as new as a baby's bottom.

Next, I addressed my eyes. An eye surgeon recommended a procedure called blepharoplasty, where she would remove excess skin, muscle,and fat around the eyes. It was outpatient surgery, so how bad could it be? With a bit of luck and a pair of dark glasses I would be as good as new in no time. It sounded good. I handed over another $3,000 dollars. The day of surgery arrived and my husband brought me to the clinic. The procedure was relatively painless because they spent 45 minutes numbing me around the eyes. I came through it without complication, got followup directions, and was escorted into the waiting room.

My husband raised his eyebrows. "You stay right here. I will get the car."

I waited in the vestibule while he got our car. He parked it, escorted me from the clinic, and helped me into the passenger seat. Then he got back in the driver's seat.

I felt a trickle of body fluid drip down my cheek and wiped it with a tissue. Then I reached up to turn down the visor and take a look.

"Don't look at it!" my husband said. "It's bad."

I couldn't resist. I turned down the visor, opened the mirror, and stared at my face. I looked like I had gone a round with Mike Tyson and lost. "Why didn't you tell me I looked like this?" I asked, once again.

This time, he stayed silent.

It took a week before I looked human. I had to wear dark glasses most of the time. Young children feared me. Strange women offered to take me to a battered women's shelter. I insisted to all that my husband wasn't beating me.   Eventually, I was healed and looked ten years younger.

Moral of the story? Beware the lighted magnifying mirror! It cost me twenty dollars. But in reality it cost me $5,000 dollars.

Clothes Shopping in the Middle Years

My word! It is devastating to my ego to shop for a dress for a fancy affair. You know, like for an important party or my son's wedding. The silouette in the department store three-way-mirror is hard to accept. Wide open necks, gray, pale pink in silk, satin, or lace are nice enough to bury my grandmother for viewing in a casket. But they are not for me! The prices started at $150.00 dollars. That would stress my budget.

I wanted a more youthful look, so I decided to get back to basics and get some new undergarments. I needed a better bra so my profile in the wedding pictures would be flattering.

Sitting naked to the waist in a chair in the 'Intimate Apparel Department', I wondered, "How do you put your bosom front and center when one breast is going east and the other is going west?" Worst of all, my stomach bulged out meeting my boobs on their way south. My twenty-three inch waist of long ago had disappeared after nursing two babies.

I looked in the full length mirror in the dressing room. My breasts resembled two bags of marbles suspended from my shoulders and crowding under my arm pits. Oh, well. I tried on a new 38D bra to see if it would help. Much to my dismay, the bottom of the cups were full and the tops were nearly empty. I had a gap so big that I could drop a tennis ball in the middle. I threw on my blouse and left the dressing room to show my girl friend.

"Look Betty Jean, this bra has shop lifting possiblities! There is a four inch gap in the middle!"

We laughted so loud and long that the sales assistant appeared. "What's so funny, ladies?"

I showed her the gap. "How can I go to my son's wedding like this?" I returned to the dressing room and abandoned the bra. I eventually found something for the wedding.

Now, when I walk fast my bosom sways from left to right. Everything up front jiggles. Nothing short of surgery will correct it. As I age, it becomes less important. I have accepted my fate!

God Wants Your Trash

Aging sometimes means we have to down size the accumulation of a lifetime. One day while having daily prayer, I reminded the Almighty how poor I was! With an overpowering awareness of God's presence, He convinced me of how rich I really was. I argued back until I took a long look into my attic, garage, closet, and cellar. Actually, I wasn't a very good steward of my possessions.

I had enough baby furniture to outfit a complete nursery. I prayed and asked the Lord who needed it. Three phone calls later it was gone to a needy family.

While doing dishes I began thinking about an almost new diaper pail and some baby clothing I had saved. One week later a young couple in my church who were between jobs were thrilled with my used items.

The Easter season was approaching. I removed from my crammed attic twelve Easter baskets, basket grass

34

and stuffed animals. Off they went to a children's mission serving the inner city. I kept rediscovering things I didn't need want or use any more.

Pages of dog food coupons were mailed to me. I gave them to a crippled neighbor whose daily companionship of her dog means a great deal to her.

My thirty-year-old doll clothes, what a treasure from the past. These things would delight some little girl's heart. So, I washed and dressed all the naked dolls I found in our church nursery.

Old glass bottles jelly jars and canning jars went to a Glass Recycling Depot. Flowerpots, empty planters went to a nursery that filled them with plants to be donated to a town library. Artificial flowers, how I detest them. Off they went to a cooperative nursery school.

Odds and ends of tape ribbon, cookie tins, and scrap cloth went to a new nursing home for crafts for elderly patients.

Berry boxes, bushel baskets, and plastic cider jugs went to a truck farmer at a roadside stand. He was a stranger to me when I started emptying my car trunk. His dark eyes glared at me. His dentures slipped down when his mouth fell open. By the time I drove away he was smiling.

Why do I cling to things? Does it give me a feeling of security? Does all this stuff have an emotional value to me?

My endless knickknacks! These dust catchers went to a flea market to raise money for a Christian day school in Buffalo, New York.

I had a brown coat I hadn't worn for three years. Through a coincidence, I met a young wife of a student pastor. She loved the coat. It gave her the warmth of encouragement. She and her husband looked forward to a life of service in the church.

What happiness I experienced making other people happy! Over the years, the deceitfulness of riches and the lust for buying and saving stuff had entered my life.

Now I have a new determination to travel light through this world and twice a year cut down on the accumulation.

Two old bikes, three pairs of shoes, six used rugs, and God had someone show up who needed them.

My life is richer because I got rid of my trash. Soon I had to move into a different community. God repaid my kindness. He brought to my new home helpful people with helpful information and opportunities.

A Moving Experience

Moving is a difficult part of life. I wouldn't wish it on my worst enemy. I moved fourteen times in my short life. That's too many!

My husband Richard was an Elder in the United Methodist Church. When your husband's boss says you're moving, you GO! Pay raises and promotions depend upon it.

My first task was always to enlist my kids and their friends to bring empty boxes home from the supermarket. But the best boxes were liquor store boxes - sturdy with lots of dividers. These boxes never failed to create the wrong impression about my husband, who took a life long vow of abstinence from alcoholic beverages. One moving day, a clutch of three ladies walked their dogs past my house, chuckling as liquor boxes were stacked in my driveway.

Part of the pain of moving is rediscovering what I hadn't returned from old moves - borrowed items and overdue library books. Oh, well.

Selling and giving away stuff brought interesting people to my door. Making appointments for donation pickups and sales was a challenge. One memorable day, I expected appointments at 10AM, noon, and 2 PM. The parties all showed up at noon, some of them looking like derelicts. They sat in their trucks, stood on my porch, and parked in my driveway competing for my attention.

"We're early by two hours, Mrs. Ives. I'm sure you don't mind. Our first stop canceled."

How could I be so lucky?

Our worst move occured when we pulled up to our new home and spotted a strange moving van. "Whose truck is that, Richard?" I cried. "It's not ours! Oh my God! No! No! No! They're moving out today. Who screwed this up?"

After six phone calls and much debate, we moved in the front door while the current occupants moved out the back. Then it began to rain. The children were cranky. I started to cry.

I started to yell when I saw my mattresses sitting outside under a tree in the rain.

The movers argued amongst themselves. "Fred, why didn't you cover them when you moved them there!" "Sorry about that Mrs. Ives, I'll cover them with a tarp." "I hope you have to sleep in a wet bed tonight, Fred!"

During another terrible move, my work crew tried to walk off the job because of a baseball game. A man argued, "It's a playoff game with a rival team. We just have to be there, Mrs. Ives!"

"But you're not done!" I cried. " I'm not sleeping on my sofa tonight in your truck!" I began to yell, "I'll sue you guys!"

I called the moving company, which fired the crew for abandoning us. We waited an hour for another crew to show up and finish the job. They worked until 11:05 P. M. That move should have been free because a load of funiture, a piano, and our office files were still at the old address . It turned into a two day move. What fun.....

***

I'm past seventy now and living in an apartment. I hope the Lord takes me in my sleep. My next move is to a casket!

True Grit

There was a new gal in town. Maggie McGee was a middle-aged, recently divorced woman trying to make her way in the world.

From behind gleaming white counters, I watched Maggie frantically wait on the 10:30 AM coffee crowd at our town diner. The room echoed with arrows of stinging words directed at her from an unhappy trio of retired men.

Ted shifted his bean bag body on a counter stool. "Hey, you! I want a refill."

The door blew shut, then opened with a bang. Maggie's arm jerked in surprise, splashing Ted and the counter with hot coffee.

Ted sprang up, cursing Maggie. "Woman, you're a slob! How do you keep a job? I want another cup!"

"So sorry… Did I burn you? I'll get a clean cup." Maggie dabbed her cloth toward his shirt and he shrieked like a banshee.

"Don't touch me you fat ass! I will take care of it myself."

With tears in her eyes, Maggie stroked her gray hair out of her face. It had escaped from a too high ponytail at the back of her head. The din of chatter resumed as she cleaned up the mess. Her nervous sweaty fingers clutched the battered metal tray. Then she headed for the kitchen.

Other customers pretended to be absorbed in conversation or their newspapers.

A few minutes later, after regaining her composure, Maggie returned and approached Joe. "How about you? Want yours warmed up?"

Joe stared beyond her.

With a smirk Fred yelled, "He doesn't talk to people he don't like."

"I'll serve him anyway," she said. Her sad tired eyes smiled at me across the room.

I smiled back at her in recognition of yet another human being in trouble. I suspected that Maggie was too young for pension, health insurance benefits, or Social Security. But she had few skills to take care of herself.

One by one Maggie's tormenters left.

"Why do you put up with these characters?" I asked.

"In time they'll accept me." Maggie's smile lit up her plump face. "This is my third day. I'm going to win this battle.

She was right. Three weeks later, the old codgers were practically eating out of her hand.

Senior Citizens Texting Guide

ATD – At the Doctors

BFF – Best Friend Fell

BTW – Bring the Wheelchair

BYOT – Bring Your Own Teeth

FWIW – Forget Where I Was

GGPBL – Gotta Go Pacemaker Battery Low

GHA – Got Heartburn Again

IMHO – Is My Hearing Aid On?

OMMR – On My Massage Recliner

OMSG – Oh My! Sorry, Gas.

ROFLACGU – Rolling on Floor and Can't Get Up

TTYL – Talk to Ya Louder

Courtesy of Facebook.com/Yourreasontolaugh2011

The 'Cat in the Hat' on Aging

I cannot see
I cannot pee
I cannot chew
I cannot screw
Oh my God, what can i do?

My memory shrinks
My hearing stinks
No sense of smell
I look like hell
My mood is bad – can you tell?

My body's drooping
Have trouble pooping
The Golden Years have come at last
The Golden Years can kiss my ass.

Courtesy of Facebook.com/Yourreasontolaugh2011
The 'Cat in the Hat' is a trademark of Dr. Seuss

Coping with Adult Children

The Eagle has Flown

In 1983 I was in limbo! The phone didn't ring, the house stayed clean, and it was too quiet.

The door to my son Rick's room yawned open without the drone of muttered phrases of Spanish class or the head spitting noise he called music.

I missed the running feet in the halls and on stairs, and the insistent ringing of the door bell, as Rick's' friends arrived to troop around the neighborhood selling magazines for new band uniforms.

There was no one to tell me how beautiful I was or that my pie was superb, with a quick follow-up request to borrow my car for a big date that weekend.

Did I miss a tornado in my life? A source of trouble and aggravation! There were no 11 p.m. requests to mend a wrestling uniform to be ready at 7:30 A.M. the next day. No demands at 9:30 P.M., for a bag lunch for an out of town soccer match, when there was nothing in the refrigerator but a red onion.

The angry discussions ceased over who devoured the tray of brownies meant for expected guests. I can't find dried ice cream spots on the kitchen counter. I don't miss a permanent sticky black spot in front of the refrigerator door from his drinking milk out of the cartoon. I was no longer afflicted with the over powering aroma of dirty gym clothes and wet track shoes when I opened the truck of my car.

Like a mother eagle, I removed the lining of feathers in the bottom of the home nest. As my eaglet felt the thorns of reality and disappointment, he sensed discomfort. Would Rick try his wings, by taking on more responsibilities? I hoped so!

One week, I pulled into my driveway to discover he had sublet his lawn job to a neighbor's kid, for half the price! When confronted, he wailed, *"Mom, tomorrow as my share of the senior class trip to Toronto I need $82.00...*

49

OK? Will you have a check ready? Uh... But...Why do I

have to earn all of it?"

It was too late to make suggestions, correct his table manners, or teach him self-discipline. What was done was done. The die was cast! Lord, had I failed him?

The severed ties were final as he reached for independence. I wondered what his thoughts were as he raced toward the future with exciting plans.

In bygone days, I was the center of his universe. The brown-eyed towhead would reach out for my hand to cross the street. The time had come to grow away from each other and this was meant to be. The process wrenched at the strings of my heart. He didn't need me anymore.

I was stagnating while my fledgling eagle soared beyond my reach. He needed me less and seldom asked for advice. Our food costs tumbled, but our phone bill was enormous.

I thought about the passage of life from one generation of eagles to another. Did I flee the nest of my parents with such glee and cool detachment?

Perhaps, I did.

Booting Up Mom

As a youngish widow, it became abundantly clear that neither of my single adult sons wanted to get stuck taking care of their "old lady" for the next 30 years. I didn't have to look for a husband. My sons started doing it for me.

They tried very hard not to be too obvious about the fact that they were trying to sharpen up the old gal like an older model car in a used car lot. Rick and Andrew thought that a change of tires, a new paint job, and some new upholstery would prepare me for the marriage market.

My 23-year-old son Andrew came home after three years in the army. One day I caught him checking me out. "Ma, did you ever think that maybe, just maybe, you need a more youthful profile? It might help you to get some dates…." There was a long pause. "Have you thought about those new fangled bras?" Another pause. "You know, for yourself... I bet they'd put your assets up front, so to speak."

"Andrew," I said, "My ample bosom would be spilling out the top."

"Well ah..." he said slowly. "It's just a thought. I want you to look nice." His voice trailed off. Discouraged, he turned away and said over his shoulder, "Never mind, it was just a suggestion."

On Mother's Day, my eldest son Richard called from Kansas City. "Hi, Ma. Guess what? I'm going to get you a year's membership in a health club for Mother's Day. Curves for Woman, or Gold's Gym. You'll drop a few pounds in no time and feel and look great! Think Ma, a real makeover for you!

"Rick, you know I detest exercise!"

"How about some dancing lessons? You need to get out once in a while, Ma."

"Drop dead and give me a rest, Ricky please."

Two weeks later, Andrew tried again. He glanced down at my uncombed hair sticking out in six directions from the top of my favorite purple coffee-stained bathrobe. "Ma, there's a coupon in the newspaper for a hair permanent at Penny's Department Store. How about getting your hair fixed up? I'll teach you some line dances and take you out to Howdy's some night. Who knows what might happen?"

Pouring another cup of coffee, I slammed the pot down and said. "Why don't you go to Howdy's, meet someone nice, marry, and make me a grandma?" That shut him up for about a week!

Three days later, a prepaid ticket for a five-minute dating mixer night at a local restaurant arrived in the mail from an "unknown source."

Two weeks later, Rick was on the phone again. "Ma, Andrew and I love you so much we want to do something really special for you this year. We will pay half your fare if you and Lois want to go on one of those singles cruises. You can't beat that offer! What do you think?"

"Richard, I just…"

"Don't say a word. Just think of what a wonderful time you'll have…"

My ire got up. "I've had it with you two guys! Why won't you just leave me alone! Or better yet… go ahead let the whole world know. Why don't you put a sign on the front lawn or on Route 33?"

"Available - a likeable mature Mom. 54,000 miles. She is a good cook, enjoys dancing and music. Original upholstery is slipping, but she's good for another 20,000 miles. Please contact the Ives Guys at…"

Andrew and Rick haven't given up! Their current kick is to sign me up for a Singles Club for widows!

A Fur Coat for Christmas

Before Christmas of 1995 in Charlotte, North Carolina, a conversation between my single adult sons happened something like this…

My youngest son Andrew called his brother. "How's my buddy and brother Rick doing? Have you finished Christmas shopping? I got a great idea! Mother loves fur, so let's surprise her with a fur coat. I was wandering around a thrift store looking for cheap jeans, when I saw this white fur jacket for $100.00."

"That's unbelievable!"

"What do you think? We each could go halves. I'll get it, and find a girlfriend to wrap it so it looks real snazzy."

"I don't know," said my oldest Rick. "Are you sure it would fit and the color is OK?"

"Yea, it'll fit her. I'll get it today."

"Great! She'll be real surprised and pleased. See you in 4 days bro... bye now."

***

My sons were close in age and working entry-level first jobs. They could barely pay rent and car payments, so airline tickets home were out of the question, until now.

We met Christmas Eve at the Charlotte Airport. We hadn't seen each other for over a year. After a candlelight worship service at a nearby church, we gathered at my son's apartment for gift giving. I was enjoying some hot cider when I was presented with an enormous box covered with ribbons and colored streamers that reflected the Christmas lights in the room.

I opened the box and slipped on the cozy white rabbit jacket. I hooted and shouted my delight, then jumped up and down and hugged my family. I was so happy that they cared enough to buy it, perhaps on time payments.

My first clue that something could go wrong was when I flipped it over my shoulder and saw the embroidered initials of the original owner. *That's all right,* I told myself. *There are lots of good used furs available. They wouldn't have the money for a new one.*

Our week together was full. One morning I flung my handbag over my arm and felt the fur seam give in the shoulder. I quickly grabbed the scissors, disappeared into the bathroom, ripped open the lining, and mended it with duct tape. The bunny pelts were dried out and tearing apart. I would just wear it this week, so I wouldn't hurt their feelings.

The next day we visited friends. I sat for hours on a black suede couch enjoying the music, food, fireplace and lovely-decorated home. When I got up to leave and thank my hostess, I saw an alarmed expression cross Rick's face and turned to see a white haired silhouette on the black sofa. I put a finger over my lips to signal him to be quiet! I didn't want Christmas spoiled for my guys.

The next day we shopped the Christmas sales and I bent over to reach some packages that slipped to the floor. Rippppp… I turned around quick but standing behind me they heard and saw it. The back was split open with a two feet gap of exposed lining, and my genuine rabbit coat was ruined.

I tried to make light of it as a joke. "Oh look what I did! I'll have it repaired at home." But my guys realized that the jacket was beyond redemption.

I'll always remember that special gift. Their good intentions backfired but it demonstrated the love of my family and their genuine attempts to make me happy at Christmas time.

The Art of Saying No

"Mom, I've just got to have a boom box! Would you help me?" pleaded Andrew.

"That's not the average birthday gift. That's a save your money and buy it item," I replied in a soft voice. "How about helping me wash eighteen windows on Saturday for $20? What do you say to that?"

"Well uh…on Saturday Paul and I were going to play some basketball with the other guys," sputtered Andrew.

How to handle a routine request for money from our children is a dilemma parents and grandparents face. I began to ask around how others faced this on going problem.

A widow named Marge, who lives on a Social Security check, told me, "I have a pat answer for everyone because of my restricted income,' she explained. 'I wish I could but I can't.' is my answer to all of them! The first time is the hardest. I would never deny myself anything to help the kids,' she continued. "You can say no and still have a good relationship."

A man named Henry says, stroking his gray white beard, "Saying no to requests for money is a gift of independence I give my children,"

A high spirited great-grandmother named Ruth says, "Don't try to match or treat children alike. It's impossible! Their ages, talents, interests, and opportunities will never be the same. You can only do this in a final will or trust fund."

George, a retired railroad engineer, has a family of five children. He keeps records of any loans in a book. If there is an estate left, his will declares that loan debt will be subtracted from their fair share.

The resourceful Edward Reid Anger family has a revolving loan fund. As each child leaves home and receives help, they in turn, must repay the fund and help the next child.

"A gift of money is not what your kids need", says Mrs. Betty Jean Marks, "The greatest thing you can give is your time. Your memories, your wealth of experience, and wisdom are precious. Your legacy is in the non-material things such as honesty and caring for others."

One hot afternoon I over heard a conversation among my neighbors. "What are you doing tonight Mike? Watching the idiot box again?" yelled Harold my neighbor across the backyards.

"No," said a grinning Mike. "Helen and I are looking at travel brochures. We have what it takes for a cruise since we learned to say no!"

On My Own

Living Alone is not a Curse

Living alone is not a curse! Some folks who live alone feel it's a hardship.

Actually it's being freed up to do your own thing. I am fortunate that I have absolute freedom to eat crackers in bed or read half the night. If you don't feel like cooking, dining on hard-boiled eggs, cheese, and yogurt is a real possibility if you live alone.

There are more opportunities to help others. There is no one coming home, to say, "Why did you do that?"

Occasionally when I feel frisky, I'm gone!

My brother Dan says, "I'm going to quit calling you. You're never home!"

"There is nobody to be home for," I replied. I don't have to wrap my life around someone else's timetable.

After an outing I feel stimulated. I'm on a roll. So I give into sudden impulses to wander around an interesting gift shop, stop and visit an old

64

friend, or have an early catfish dinner at four thirty because I'm in the neighborhood of the best fish market in Buffalo.

I stop to shop at my favorite places – the bakery, antique shop, book store, and ice cream parlor.

Living alone means you don't have to keep your clothes on. One blistering hot day a delivery man was surprised, when I showed up at the front door wearing just hair curlers, a halter and short shorts.

I clean only when company is coming. I wash clothes once a month. Whenever I feel lonely, I call someone who is also alone. Then I offer to help them with painting, gardening, or packing to move.

Solitude has enriched my life. I enjoy the moment! I have time to listen to my neighbor's

WW II stories or look though old picture albums. I sit and watch the snow fall as twilight blurs into total darkness.

Sometimes I rearrange my furniture twice in one week or decide not to answer the phone. When things go wrong, I pound on my organ or curse at my canary. I pick my own concert tickets, TV programs, and clubs I want to be a part of.

I'm alone and free to do the things I have longed to do for years! Hurrah!

Dates From Hell

I was introduced to the world of singles after being widowed four years. I was ready to date a knight in shining armor My matchmaking friends invited me to a Labor Day weekend party at Loon Lake, New York.

Soon after arriving I was enticed to take a canoe ride with a mature gentleman artist my age. Out and back was a relaxing ride. As we approached the shore, I leaned to the left to pick a huge water lily, inches from my grasp. The canoe tipped over amid the laughter of other guests. My $32 spiffy hairdo was gone. I surfaced looking like a drowned muskrat, with seaweed hanging off my nose and shoulders. Recovering in someone else's clothes, I decided it was just a poor start.

One summer in Sanborn, a nice guy hung around my garage sale. Bluntly he said "Would you like to go fishing with me? But, I was wondering, how old are you?"

I replied.

"Fifty four? Forget it, lady I'm only 44. Sorry!"

It was no great loss. I hate the smell of cleaning fish.

Sometime later, a friend I met at a conference said, "If you ever get near Pittsburgh call me."

Getting up the nerve to phone him took courage. I headed for his remote place, dreaming of a lovely afternoon getting to know a fine man.

While we toured his property, Ned's Saint Bernard Duke repeatedly wedged himself between us. When I touched Ned's arm, Duke growled. This amused my friend. When the phone rang, the dog chased me to a screened porch, where I ate lunch alone. When I left, Duke raced me to my car down a lane. I leaped into the front seat before the dog could nip at my ankles.

"He's already married," I muttered to myself. "I can't compete with Duke."

Double Divorced Don came my way. Over dinner I hear of his recent heartaches. I wanted to scream: "Let me out of here!"

After a lovely supper together, my new date drove us to a cemetery for some serious cuddling. We walked around the moonlight paths listening to nightingales. Returning to the car, we were surprised to find instructions to call the Sheriff's Department because we were locked in for the night. The public phone required quarters or a phone card. Neither of us had a cell phone or quarters. An argument developed over whose fault it was.

I finally dumped out the contents of my purse and discovered a 2-year old Amtrak phone card. We called, the trooper said that we would have to wait. There were graduation parties all over the county so it might be two hours.

It seemed appropriate that I was stuck in a cemetery, because my love life was in a fatal condition.

Caught Unaware

In the fall of 2006, I visited friends in Western New York. On the way home, as I approached Mount Morris, I enjoyed the glorious array that peppered the landscape with browns, golds, oranges, and reds. It was a lovely October day.

Why run out to buy a fall arrangement for my party tonight? I thought. *There is such an abundance of autumn leaves, berries, and sumac within reach of the road.* I'll make a quick stop and cut some brush for a fall arrangement.

I was approaching Sonyea, New York on Route #36 so I lowered my speed to a crawl. Pulling off to the right shoulder of the road, I dug out my husbands old camping knife from the glove compartment . It was made in the 1930's. Blazing sun light reflected from the pocket knife. Stepping into a ditch with waist high weeds, I began slashing at cotton tails.

70

Five minutes later, two squad cars with flashing lights and sirens blaring descended on me from opposite directions. Squealing tires cut sharply into the gravel at the side of the road. The cars parked within ten feet of my car. Two New York State Correctional Officers approached me in the ditch.

"What are you doing here, Madam?" said a thirty plus guy with a moustache.

Stunned, I glanced up and looked them over. Four tall handsome men - alert and very serious looking, all under 50 - stared menacingly at me with hard eyes.

"Am I trespassing, Sir?" I said in a sweet innocent questioning voice. "I thought weeds by the side of the road were in the public domain."

"What are you doing?"

"I'm cutting down brush to decorate my home for a party tonight. My name is Mrs...."

"Ives. We know exactly who you are!" Snapped the officer with red hair sticking out from his cap. "We had your picture and license plate on seven TV monitors before we arrived here. Mrs.Ives. You are parking within 20 yards of a high security prison and you are carrying a threatening weapon."

With fresh eyes, I gazed up across the road where acres of prison buildings, vehicles, and exercise yards were surrounded by twenty feet high fences with curly barbed wire on the top. I was outside the Groveland Correctional Facility.

"Do I look like a candidate for a prison break? I'm a senior citizen and a retired teacher! My lethal weapon is a rusty Boy Scout Camper knife."

"That may be so. But..."

"Four more bundles ought to do it, Officer."

"Ok ! Make it quick, Mrs. Ives."

Four men said nothing and returned to their cars and

sat. They never took their eyes off me. They were very serious about their jobs. They watched me pick arm loads of Chinese lanterns, greens, and bittersweet berries.

Soon, I was done. I hopped into my car, waved, and yelled out the window, "Thank you, guys! You're really on the ball safe guarding New York State residents!"

As I pulled away, I heard their car radio blare out, "Sam! Are you and your crew still in the ditch cutting weeds with that old bat? Get your butt up here right now! It's time for rounds."

Dogs!

Walking up a busy street, I found myself separated from my group of walkers. The nice houses had deep lots with manicured lawns and flowers. I approached my friends from behind – two middle-aged women and one young girl with a beautiful female Irish Setter on a leash.

Three mature male dogs - two huge adult German Shepherds and a mutt, bounded out from a porch, barking. They circled the new dog and wagged their tails, happy at the sight of a prospective mate.

The Irish Setter strained forward and broke her leash. She frolicked on the lawn with the German Shepherds.

The owner came out of the house roaring, "Why can't you ladies control your dog?" He called to his canines in a commanding voice to heel at his side. He was totally ignored. Stunned at their lack of response, he yelled

"That's alright, ladies! They won't go beyond my new electric fence."

The fence didn't work. The German Shepherds reared up and pranced forward ready to mount the female.

Suddenly, a young father and two little kids on bikes with trainer wheels came up the side walk. "Oh Daddy! Look! What are the doggies doing? I didn't know dogs could dance. They are dancing on their hind legs. What are they going to do?

The look on their father's face was worth a hundred dollars. His change of expression went from: "What the hell is gong on?' Then "Oh My God!" Then " Hurry up kids. We are late for dinner." They scurried away.

The three ladies threw themselves forward toward their dog. She eluded them and dashed away to join her new friends. At this surprise move, the ladies ended up rolling on the ground. They chased her through hedges and around trees in an attempt to catch her. They ended in a heap on the grass trying to capture and tie the dog.

One of the older women grabbed the mouth and head and got bit. "Get the muzzle on her. She's biting me. I'm bleeding!"

The owner of setter yelled, "I'm not worried about that. I'm worried about her other end."

They secured the dog by laying on top of the animal. The ladies finally controlled their dog, unscrambled themselves, stood, and straightened their hair. They found their purses and headed for the sidewalk yelling at each other.

"Why didn't you hold her tighter?" "Why did you bring her?" "She's not a puppy! You need a stronger leash for a dog that size, stupid!"

I sat on the grass and watched the charade, laughing. The women glared at me and walked away. This was one walk I won't forget!

Alphabetical Actions for Aging Gracefully

A - accept being a slower organism
B - balance your life with work and play
C - challenge yourself with new and unique experiences
D - diet - change your diet - change your life
E - enrich your environment
F - forgive others as God forgives you
G - games - play them daily
H - hone in on humor
I - intelligences - incorporate all of them
J - journal
K - keep working at what you enjoy
L - learn life long
M - memory - sharpen yours daily
N - novelty - do at least one thing differently each day
O - optimism - see the glass half full
P - pray and meditate
Q - question things - ask what if? and why?
R - reduce stress
S-sing
T - travel
U - use all things in moderation
V - vitamins are a wellspring of health
W - water - it is the mainstream of life - drink up!
X - exercise - just do it!
Y - yesterdays, recall them and share your memories
Z - zzz's catch some with a nap

Source: Barbara Bruce
'Mental Aerobics – 75 Ways to Keep Your Brain Fit'
Used with Permission

God's Protective Bubble

After the death of my husband, I got involved with 'Bridges to Education'. I was a teacher and the organization had a program to teach English as a second language to the countries of eastern Europe. Many of these were third world countries. I joined a group of American teachers on a trip to the the Slovakian Republic.

One day, I was sight seeing in Budapest with my colleagues. I wanted to leave the group and travel mid-afternoon to the border; then cross into the Slovakian Republic. This involved traveling alone and changing trains twice. I was compelled to visit young churches active since their 1991 freedom from the Soviet Union. I made plans to visit with Missionaries and visit two fledgling congregations.

People were praying for me as I traveled for hours with a cheat sheet of phrases in Hungarian and the

Slovakian Language. I was easy to identify as an American because of my red, white, and blue clothing. God put in my path friendly helpful English speaking young people. They stepped out of crowds to practice their English language skills by conversing with me. They checked my tickets and told me where the toilets were and where to eat in railroad stations along the way. Hours later, a retired couple guarded me while I slept so my luggage or I didn't disappear.

When I reached the border crossing into Slovakia , the Lord provided a guardian angel in the form of a huge Norwegian College kid named Hans. This guy was built and dressed like a Viking who had just stepped out of the pages of a book. He sat beside me and smoked cigarettes. This made me nervous. I feared his stubby cigarettes would cause his curly blond beard to catch on fire. We talked all night about his home, his girlfriends, and his future plans. I asked Hans what he thought was the meaning of life. He said he wasn't very religious. He said to have a good time and do good when you can. He'd worry about God when he was dying.

Approaching the border, the guards on the train insisted that I pay a tax to leave Hungary to cross the border. I had no Hungarian money left.

"They won't accept Slovakian money or a credit card. What can I do Hans?" Looking up at his six foot two inch frame I frowned at him.

Under his breath he whispered, "They want American money. How much cash do you have?"

"Thirteen dollars in one dollar bills."

"Give it to me." My Viking rose and walked up the isle. His head just cleared the doorway at the end of the rail road car. "This is all the American lady has in U.S. Dollars!" Hans loudly addressed the three-border patrol that stopped the train. He threw a fistful of American dollars up in the air. "I'm sure it is enough. Now leave her alone!"

Toting semi-automatic rifles, the three small-framed border guards in gray baggy uniforms collected the money. They chatted among themselves in Hungarian. Then they nodded their heads up and down. Yes! I could pass.

With a boyish grin on his face, Hans returned to his seat beside me and promptly fell asleep.

On that trip, I felt I was traveling in an insulated bubble of God's protection. In the customs line at Nitra, in the Slovakia Republic, I was surrounded by a group of ten students. The Railroad Security Guards were searching everyone's suitcases, hand luggage, purses, and pockets without exception for drugs. I was not even asked to declare what I brought into Slovakia.

In the Slovakian Republic, I spoke through a translator sentence by sentence to those assembled. When I returned home to America, I witnessed to God's power and protection to various groups and the miracles the Lord was doing in peoples' lives.

Since then, every time I doubt God's leading and enabling strength, I remind myself that we are consistently in God's presence and protective care.

A Woman's Intuition

Too Young To Be Hitch Hiking

In the early seventies, I was taking my kids for a walk. Three times I got this strong impression of words coming to my mind. "Get in the car. Someone needs you."

I put my kids in the car and handed them a sucker.

"Where are we going Mommy?" asked Ricky.

" Ah... We will see," I replied.

I got on the thruway entrance toward Hamburg. Nothing remarkable came to my attention, so I kept driving. In early afternoon there is not much traffic. The miles rolled by, and I berated myself. *What am I doing here? You must be nuts! Such a reckless impulsive thing to do. A u-turn at the next opportunity is a good idea.* Then I saw her. A teenager girl in a thin cotton shift plastered to her cold wet body was hitch hiking in the rain and wind. Her long black hair blow across her face and tangled with her shoulder strap of her purse. I stopped.

Her name was Brenda. The girl was hysterical, sobbing, and shivering.

I handed Brenda tissues introduced and tried to calm her, while I put on the heat. Her story gushed out of her. After a fight with her mother, Brenda stormed out. Her car ran out of gas on the thruway, so she started walking.

I took her to a rest stop and ordered hot chocolate. My kids were restless. I needed to get home for a couples club I was hosting at my house. I gently suggested that she contact her family and she did.

Brenda returned from the pay phone. "You don't need to wait. My older brother will pick me up soon."

Twenty minutes later, we parted. I watched her get into her brother's car and drive away.

To this this day, I wonder if she would have suffered, if I hadn't come across her that day. I am glad that I listened to my inner prompting.

When In Doubt, Don't

In the mid-eighties, my husband Richard stopped the car and I hopped out into a four-foot-square puddle. Muddy water oozed out of my new open-toed size five shoes as I stood on the street corner in our small city.

Out in the rain, I didn't feel so brave. Rain dripped off my rain hood and trickled down my back. Walking several blocks of wet pavement had put a fine spray of dirty water on the back of my legs. I looked and feel like a drowned rat. My hands were cold. My feet were wet. My petite frame was bent into the wind. A sudden gust turned my red umbrella inside out, so I trashed it in a sidewalk container.

With a sigh of relief, I noticed that the New Commons was finally in sight. "Fourteen Boutiques," boasted the yellow flashing sign to a deserted street. Suddenly the building seemed sinister as I sensed something evil about it. The brickwork was grimy. On the second floor were two window shades pulled halfway down, giving the appearance of two half-closed eyes.

The doors were propped open like a gaping mouth with a black interior. In front of the four front doors, a huge green mat spread from the entrance to the curb, looking like a protruding tongue.

"What an imagination", I scolded myself. "I must be crazy. Why would a newly decorated structure appear like an evil human face?"

An untidy bag lady stepped out of a narrow doorway clutching her belongings close to her body. The sour aroma of her presence lingered. I crossed the street and headed toward the entrance of the building. Strong words of warning entered my mind, "Don't go in there!"

"Why not? It's the only dry place to shop." I glanced at my watch. It was two twenty on a Tuesday afternoon. I stepped toward the entrance, seeking a restroom.

Again, the inner voice prodded me, "Don't go in there!" Doubtfully, I stood looking around. I didn't doubt the source of the message, but I didn't want to obey and revise my plans. A shiver of apprehension had me undecided. What was I to do? Two and one half hours with nothing to do...I was now trembling with cold.

Conflicting feelings chased through my mind, "Why shouldn't I enjoy myself with lunch and shopping? I'm starved." With rain pelting my face, I decided not to go into the Commons.

"When in doubt, don't."

With fresh purpose, I turned and headed for a diner and warmed up with two hot dogs and hot chocolate. "Which way to the library, Sir?" I asked of the potbellied cook whose long dirty apron strings danced when he walked. His unsavory glance undressed me as he decided my income and age.

"Let me see," he said, wiping his hands on the back

of his pants, "West four blocks and north two."

"I have an hour to kill before my husband picks me up."

"Lady, why don't you go to the Commons to shop? You would be safe and dry there. Walking to the library isn't the best idea in this neighborhood."

"I have my doubts about going to the Commons, so that's not for me today. Thanks for the directions."

At 4:30, my smiling middle-aged husband pulled up in front of the bank. "You drive," he instructed as he slid to the passenger seat. Then with an astonished look, he queried, "What, no packages?"

"I had a strange and lonely quiet afternoon all by myself. Things didn't turn out." I glanced his way and saw that he was asleep. How could he? I fumed! Sleeping on my time when this was the only privacy we ever had in our household. Disappointed, I drove home through the gathering dusk, which enfolded the hills around our parsonage.

The following evening, browsing through the daily paper, I was stunned when I read: "At approximately 2:30 Tuesday a woman was raped in the restroom at the Commons on the second floor of the new shopping boutique. Anyone who saw anything suspicious in the vicinity of the restaurant, please call the police department at..."

"Richard!" I leaped off the sofa. "Richard!"

"What's up?" he shouted from three rooms away.

"I can't believe this. Read this!" Shaking, I handed him the newspaper and dropped into a chair. "That poor woman! Oh, Richard. It could have been me! I was at the Commons at two-twenty. God spared me the humiliation and terror of being a victim of rape. I heard my Shepherd's voice, 'Don't go in there.'"

Richard clasped me in a giant hug. "Thank God for His protection."

Helping People

Life in the Slow Lane

Not too long ago, I had major surgery and was told to recuperate for six weeks. I asked myself, "Am I trapped or am I free?"

I decided that I was free to grow and develop a new dimension of living. It was an opportunity not given to everyone. Suddenly my days were not measured by a stopwatch; there was a more even pace. There was time to read, rest, and relax. I looked for chances to explore my world and use time wisely. Boredom, self pity, and depression would not happen to me!

Basking in the love and concern showered on me by family and friends, I was the center of attention. It was part of the therapy of coming home from the hospital. But I soon learned that few people wanted to hear every detail of my colossal experience - what the doctor said on Tuesday, my difficulties with the blonde nurse, what the therapist said. It was of no interest to the average inquirer who said, "How are you doing?"

I was responsible for my own entertainment. I had time to do all the things I never had time for before. So, I sorted vacation pictures, looked at old year books and scrap books, and reviewed my children's wedding albums.

After a few days, I asked, "How many people do I owe letters or e-mails to?" I set up a list and made every Monday a write, call, or e-mail day. I contacted people from days gone by - a coworker, a distant relative, neighbor, or a friend facing life alone. Renewing these ties with dear ones brought joy and immense satisfaction. Then I asked how others coped with healing time.

My neighbor Martha dug out January sale Christmas cards and addressed them for the next holiday. Recuperating from her broken leg gave her the time to write a newsy note on each one.

My Aunt Melrose kept busy after a hysterectomy

making layettes for newborn babies. Her sewing skills and craftsmanship paid off. She now takes orders and has a supplementary income.

Ralph, recovering from open-heart surgery, had a sudden whim to send away to a mail order house for a grandfather clock kit. The man suddenly had a reason to get up in the morning. He worked in short periods from twenty minutes to one hour, assembling the grandfather clock. He bought more kits and busily assembled clocks for months. My friend used three clocks as Christmas gifts for family members and sold five on consignment at a gift shop.

A friend recovering from surgery almost got divorced when he occupied his time alphabetizing his wife's canned goods!

After a few weeks, I was starting to feel better. I thought that I was ready for company, so I invited over one friend a week to teach me a new skill, such as knitting, chess, or a card game. I had to limit their visit to two hours and say, "I've had it for today, I really must nap now."

After a month, I was afraid that my mind was turning to jelly. I considered taking a correspondence course or studying a foreign language. Nothing appealed to me. I watched television while performing other tasks - sorting manufacturer's coupons, polishing silver, and cleaning out the clutter in drawers.

My good intentions serviced and I began to exercise my spiritual muscles. I read two books of the Bible a week, starting with the shorter ones in the New Testament. I squeezed in a biography or two a week about people who did selfless things. This inspired me to pray for others.

My recovery was almost over and reflection was in order. During a time of forced inactivity, it would have been easy to bury myself in frivolous time-consumers, such as soap operas or solitaire. Thank goodness that I saw it as an opportunity to grow. It was important to be patient with myself because healing took place slowly. Time is a

precious gift, if used in meaningful ways.

Clara Barton's Second Career

After teaching elementary school for several years Clara Barton, a single 40-ish large-framed plain looking woman, decided to change the direction of her life. When the Civil war broke out, she quit her job in the Patent Office to assist the soldiers. Her first of many trips to the battle fields were met with suspicious comments from people who thought she was there as a camp follower interested in sex or marriage. She was accused of robbing the dead of valuables or keepsakes that should go the mothers, wives, or sweethearts at home.

Much of her opposition was because she was a single mid-aged women with no one to protect her. Clara in her early work had no church or organization behind her to legitimize her offers to help. Officials told her repeatedly that the battlefield was much to dangerous for a single women and she should get the hell home, pray, and knit socks if she wanted to help the wounded and dying.

Thank God she didn't listen to their threats and reminders to "Go home, woman!"

The curious, bums, beggers, and grave pickers would swarm over a battlefield as soon as the gun fire stopped to collect boots, clothing, money, or watches.

Clara perceived that she needed a sign, uniform, or form of government approval to serve the wounded at the front lines. Gradually, she earned the begrudging respect of exhausted army surgeons' approval by purchasing at her own expense wagon-loads of blankets, food, water, bandages, and what medicication she could secure.

Clara drove the horses to the front lines. Sometimes the morning light showed bullet holes in her skirts and cannon balls in the back of the wagon. Some of her horses died from wounds received during the hazardous trips.

Thousands of soldiers called her lovingly the "Angel of the Battlefield" because she brought water and comfort to the dying. Clara visited field hospitals that were quickly organized in churches, barns, town squares, or dance halls. She wrote letters home for many men.

Year after year she kept at it - making appointments with members of Congress or officials connected with the Department of Defense trying to get permanent access with out a hassle because she was not a professional nurse. She tried to help the wounded that some times laid all night in open woods, fields, or hills sides till long after the battle stopped. The army would retreat or moved forward toward the enemy's troops, walking and dragging their cannons over the bodies of the fallen.

Her friends, army doctors, church people, and folks from the surrounding towns all over America started shipping her clothing, bandages, blankets, and linens.

After the Civil War ended, she worked for years identifying remains, tracing pictures, matching clothing to identify the wounded, the dead, and 30,000 unknown soldiers. When invited to join the social whirl of

Washington D.C., she was not a striking beauty or fashion plate who would draw rich or important people to her cause. But over time, her earnests, beautiful spirit, organizational skills, and letter writing to government officials drew attention, admiration, and support.

Clara was invited to Europe to speak and visit with friends there. In Switzerland, she met the founder of the Red Cross of Europe. This changed her life again.

She returned home convinced that America needed such a national organization in peace time as well as war time. It could aid victims of floods, fires, and disasters of every kind. She knew that it had to be humanitarian, compassionate, and free from political or religious affiliation.

Clara returned to Dansville, New York and bought a house a few miles from were she was raised. Her living room became the 1st headquarters of the American Red Cross in the U.S.A. She hired a secretary and servants so she would be free to write, travel, and speak to groups to start more Red Cross Chapters across New York State and in Washington D.C.

When invited to join the social world of Dansville or Washington D.C., she declined and remained focused on her life's work, the Red Cross.

Clara Barton is a woman to emulate. If only we could all be so productive in our later years.

Heaven's Heroes

Cydel Maxwell got the worst possible news. A malignant lump was found in her right breast, requiring immediate lumpectomy surgery. This devastating fact took over her life with doctor's appointments, mammograms, biopsy, lumpectomy surgery, and recovery.

After surgery at the United Methodist Hospital in Omaha, she returned to her job as Civil Secretary of Administration to the Sheriff of Ida County, Iowa.

Sitting at her desk, she wondered, *How will I get through the workday with six weeks of radiation treatments facing me? Can I fight for my life and keep my job at the same time?*

At that moment, a burly deputy toting a gun, with mud on his boots, nonchalantly dropped paper work on Cydel's desk as he passed by. Scanning the form, Cydel thought he was claiming compensation time for a vacation. Reading it, she burst into tears. She realized the hours, sick days, and vacation time that a group of deputies were sacrificing for her.

Secretly, fellow workers had gone to their boss Sheriff Wade A. Harriman. They even called Thomas Miller the Iowa Attorney General in Branson, Iowa to secure permission to donate their hours to her record.

Five Deputies each gave her a week of their compensation time. Dave Schossow, an investigator, was a gentle giant. Mike Hawthorne was a shy young fellow who had just joined the department six months ago. Sheldon Pettit was always telling stories and jokes. Kevin Frank was a murder investigator and Tom Peterson was called the "Kindergarten Cop," because he looked like a kid. Randy Peterson gave one week of his precious vacation time.

A grand total of 240 hours gleaned from overtime that could have been paid out to them in cash. Without their help, Cydel would not have enough compensation time to cover six weeks of daily radiation treatments, and the two-hour ride roundtrip to Sioux City.

What a great bunch of guys! Ida County Deputy's motto is: "To protect and serve." These modest "noblemen" considered their generosity a part of their service to the community. But to Cydel, they were angelic heroes.

Not in Our Neighborhood

In a northern industrial city, a proud German
population was clustered on the edge of Lake Erie. Small
houses with tall narrow windows lined the crowded streets.
Workers had built this East Side section of Buffalo when
the railroads were in their prime. A hundred years had
passed and time had changed things considerably.

In the middle of the block on Sumner Place, there
lived a retired couple who was still young in spirit. They
had been married at the church across the street from them
at Sumner Place United Methodist Church. Frank and
Alberta raised a family across and lived there for over fifty
years.

Frank was short of stature with a huge belly. When
he wore a tie, his tie descended down from his neck like a
ski slope. He had snapping compelling blue eyes and a
quick temper. He was a retired driver for the Hall's Bakery
Company in Buffalo. His customers taught him how to

handle all kinds of people.

Alberta had short gray hair and a warm smile. Her contagious laughter made others laugh. She was the organist at the church for many years.

Not long ago on a hot summer evening, they endeared themselves to everyone in the neighborhood of Sumner Place. A group of kids from another neighborhood picked their street for a gang rumble. It was a muggy midsummer evening. It looked like a hot quiet sleepy neighborhood. Many people were vacationing, so some homes were vacant.

Frank and Alberta came home from their customary Friday night fish fry. As they drove down their street they realized that the crowd outside the laundromat was double the usual number. They were agitated about something. Strange kids loitered in front of the Convenience and Pizza Store one block away, armed with baseball bats and chains. Loud voices shouted threats and insults to the group gathered on the other side of the street. The street lights

reflected off tire irons and brass knuckles in their hands. At

the other end of Sumner Place, thirty or forty young people

with pipes and switchblade knives milled around waiting

for something to happen.

Frank and Alberta's mouths fell open as they

approached their home and sensed what was beginning to

happen.

"This can't happen here," sputtered Alberta, with

anger in her voice. "Not in our neighborhood, but what can

we do Frank, we don't know these kids."

"I've lived on this street for many years and nothing

like this has ever happened before, and it won't happen

now," Frank said with determination.

"I don't know if there's anything we can do about it.

We are old and alone Frank, I don't want you getting hurt

trying to be brave."

Frank drove down the street and dropped off

Alberta. Meanwhile, Alberta sat on her porch watching apprehension grow among her neighbors' faces as they peered out windows or through screen doors or perched on their porches. Fear was written on their faces. Some retreated indoors, shut their windows, and drew their curtains. They weren't going to get involved.

"Alberta. Look what's happening! What can we do?" Mrs. Blartz yelled with panic in her voice to her friend next door. "How can we disperse this group without confronting them?"

Alberta thought for a moment. "I don't know. That loud mouth sexy blond waitress could handle them. What's her name again? I don't remember. She lives two doors from Bruce's going north."

Mrs. Blartz nodded. "Maybe the fireman on the next street might help. Do you think he'd be home on a holiday? It's worth a try, I'll call him."

More people joined them, from both sides of the

street. Harold from across the street was a World War II vet. He joined the two womwn. "Ladies, let's call Gracie. Tell her there's trouble and she should bring her three big German Shepherds, without their leashes, to Frank's house right away."

"I'll call," said a meek fragile lady listening into the informal meeting.

"Who else has big dogs? Who's the guy that walks the big Irish Setter?" asked Ralph?

"What about that new cook built like a prizefighter? He works at the diner, doesn't he?" asked Frank. "He's a real walking wall. We could use him right now too. Tilly, go knock on the door with yellow shutters."

"Alberta, do you know the name of that Eagle Scout who lives upstairs from Ruth's Beauty Shop? Somebody go get him. I think he lives in the blue house."

Harold turned to a 10 year old standing near him. "Jackie honey. Grab that newspaper boy, Jeremy, that plays basketball. Would you catch him on your bike honey and bring him back quick?"

"Sure thing," she replied, peddling off.

"Hey you guys, have you two thought about how we could we try water hoses?"

"It won't work, Ralph. What if they get mad at me? I don't want to get hurt," whined a white haired lady.

Then give your hose to Mrs. Peeves' son Ralph. He's not afraid of anyone."

Ralph looked out the door and bounded down the front stairs. "Where is your hose, Lady. I'll do it!"

A look of relief flooded her face. "Oh that's wonderful! I'll call three other neighbors. Do you think I should call the police? I really don't know..."

"I'll call the police," said Alberta. "At least I can do that much. Harold, if you drag out my hose to the front of my property I'll hold the hose and turn up the valve to full force."

"O.K," said Harold. "Will do."

Alberta took on fresh hope and started yelling, "Get your garden hoses out, folks. We're going to do something about these troublesome characters! Let's cool them off."

Frank in the meantime turned his car around and started down the long street at fifty miles an hour. Then his 1987 car compiled from three other vehicles backfired. The noise and speed of his ancient secondhand red car got the kids' attention and they scattered like frightened chickens. When Frank reached the largest group at the end of Sumner Street, he brought his car to a screening halt. He jumped up shrieking like a mad man, "Get out of here! Go home! We don't want anyone around here looking for trouble."

Timid Alberta decided to stand with her neighbors after all. "I won't confront them. But I can hold a hose."

With a full hard spray, she and six other neighbors pelted everything with water: kids, parked cars, bikes, dogs, and garbage cans. Other brave residents followed their example. Nine people with hoses encircled the young people. Then, people approached with their leashed dogs, except for Gracie and her highly trained police dogs. The result was absolute bedlam.

Above the squealing and yelling as the kids were pelted by the intense spray of six garden hoses, a police siren was heard. When the police arrived, most of the youngsters had disappeared into yards and over fences, or took off on their bikes or skateboards.

Belligerent gang leaders were still trying to start an argument with the group across the street milling around.

The police rounded them up and took their weapons away.

Frank parked his car out of the way and the neighbors turned of their hoses and gathered round to talk about it on the porch. Grace tied her dogs to the railing on the front steps and sat down to rest. Frank and Alberta settled on their porch and let the police handle things.

Neighbors brought pop and cookies and spread out the food on the wide railing that ran across the porch. Next door neighbors brought over extra lawn chairs and block a party shaped up real fast. The young people dispersed and after awhile the peace and quiet of a warm June evening returned to the street.

A handsome Buffalo Police officer approached the group gathered on the porch and lawn. "I'm Lieutenant Macks. Is every one alright?" Everyone stopped talking and looked up toward the officer. There was a moment of silence. "That's good news. Which one of you is Frank?"

Frank stepped out of the group and said "I am."

The police officer grinned. "You're a brave man to tackle these hoodlums."

"Well, nobody else was around. So we old folks, Ralph, and my neighbors had to take over the situation and organize things. I didn't do much." He looked around at

113

the faces of his neighbors standing around his porch, the Boy Scout, the cook, the retired fireman, and many others. "You each played an important part here tonight," said Frank. "We couldn't have accomplished anything without each of you helping and at least doing something."

With flashing eyes Alberta said, "Nobody's going to start trouble in our neighborhood!"

Wrapup

I'm between Tampax and Depends; a mature older gal past fifty. I refuse to grow old graciously. I'm fighting it every inch of the way. I've found that humor helps us to age with class.

I hope that you have enjoyed this book!

Other Books by Bertamae

Ring in the Holidays – a collection of short stories, music, humor, gift suggestions, and techniques for surviving the holidays.

Doing Good for Goodness' Sake by Steve Zikman – Bertamae contributed a chapter titled, 'They Gave at the Office'. True stories about people making a difference in the lives of others.

Made in the USA
Charleston, SC
01 February 2012